BIG BOOK
OF
GRAPHIC DESIGNS
AND
DEVICES

by Typony Inc.

DOVER PUBLICATIONS, INC.

NEW YORK

Published in Canada by General Publishing Company,
Ltd., 30 Lesmill Road, Don Mills, Toronto, Ontario.
Published in the United Kingdom by Constable and
Company, Ltd.

This Dover edition, first published in 1990, is an un-
abridged republication of *Etcetera: Graphic Devices*, originally
published in 1980 by Van Nostrand Reinhold Company, New
York. For this edition, several pages of art have been moved
from their original positions to others, and the original table
of contents has been amended accordingly.

DOVER *Pictorial Archive* SERIES

Library of Congress Cataloging-in-Publication Data

Typony inc.
    [Etcetera, graphic devices]
    Big book of graphic designs and devices / by Typony inc.
        p.   cm. — (Dover pictorial archive series)
    Reprint. Originally published: Etcetera, graphic devices.
New York: Van Nostrand Reinhold Co., 1980.
    ISBN 0-486-26261-8
    1. Decoration and ornament—Themes, motives. I. Title.
II. Series.
NK1530.T93   1990
745.4—dc20   89-23800
                                                            CIP

·········· CONTENTS ··········

Examples using the devices	5
Floral motifs	8
Fleurs-de-lys	13
Crosses	14
Snowflakes	16
Ships	18
Anchors	20
Butterflies	22
Lions	24
Griffins	26
Nymphs	28
Crowns	30
Compasses	32
Playing card suit symbols	33
Decorative motifs	34
Decorative frames and borders	64
Suns	97
Circles	100
Ellipses	109
Squares	113
Rectangles	126
Decorative patterns	169

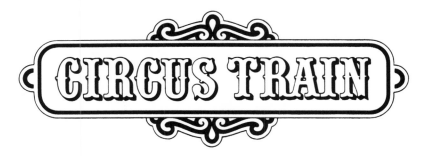

CIRCUS TRAIN

FUN

W   E

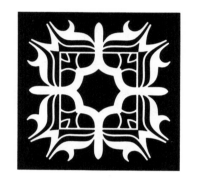

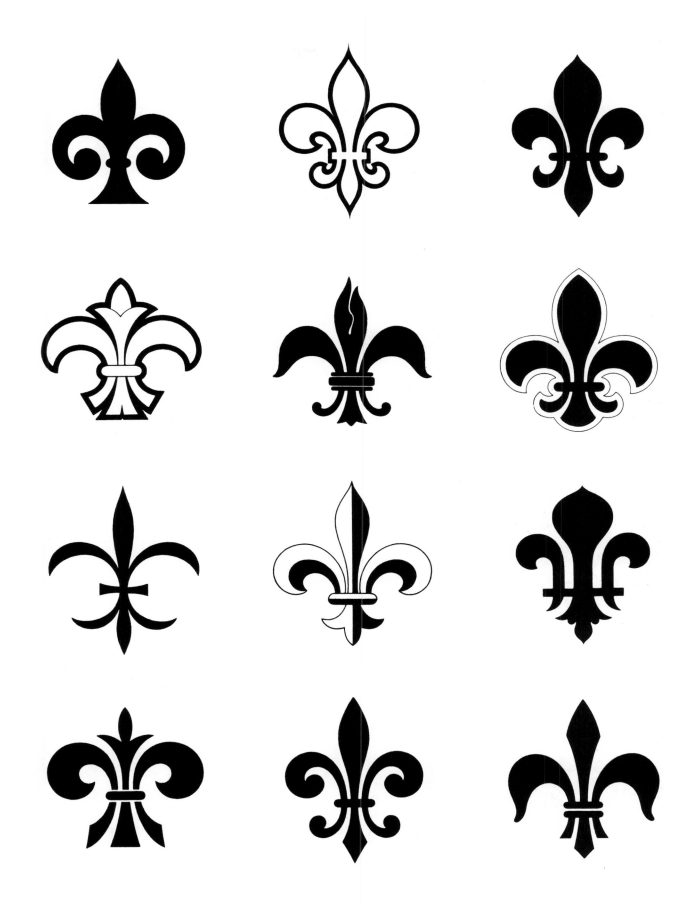

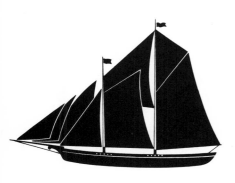  

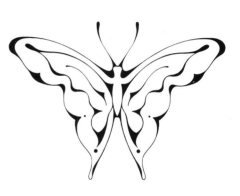

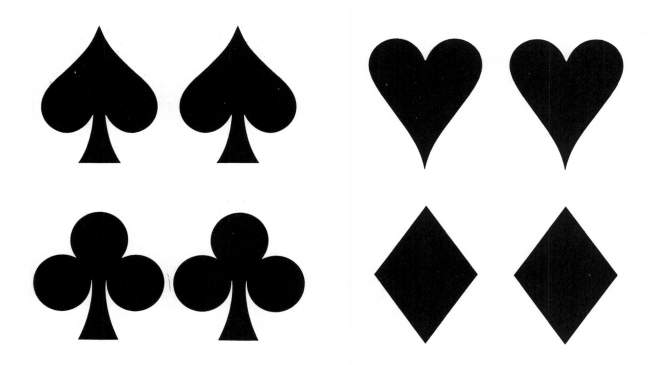

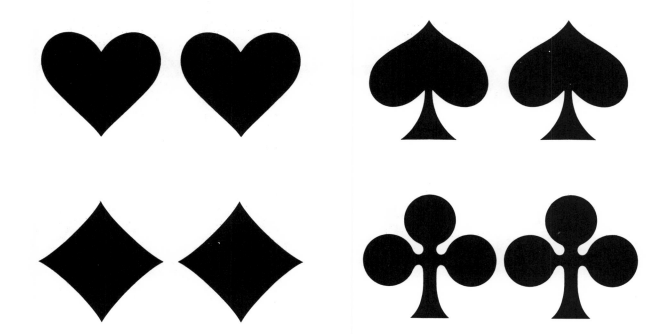

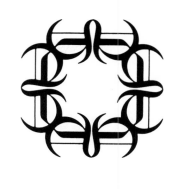

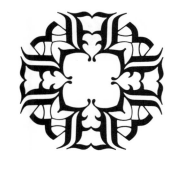

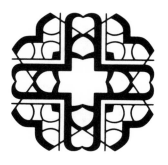

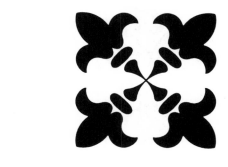

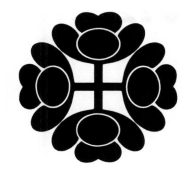

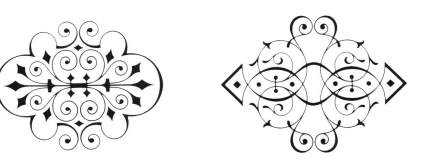

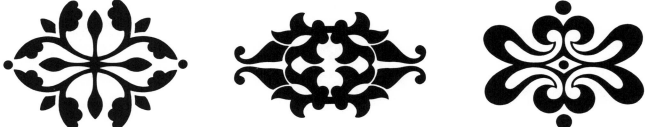

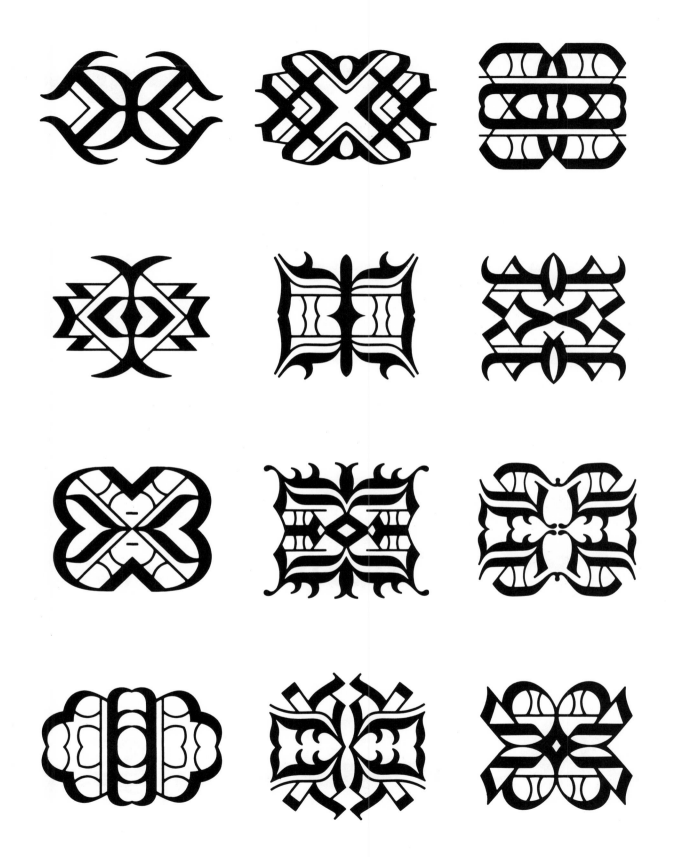

44

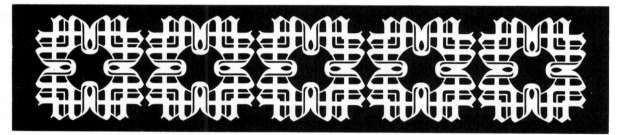

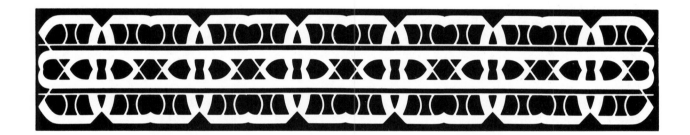

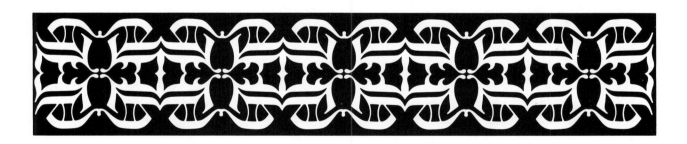

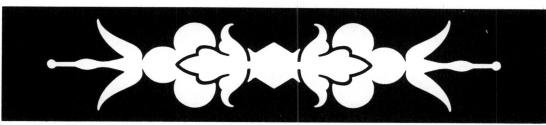

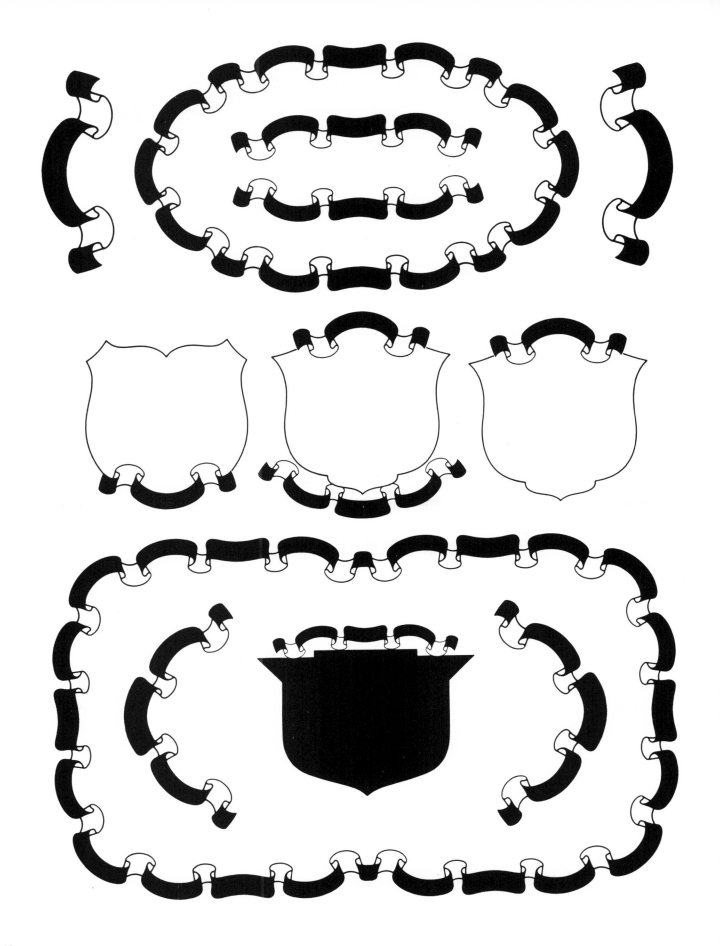

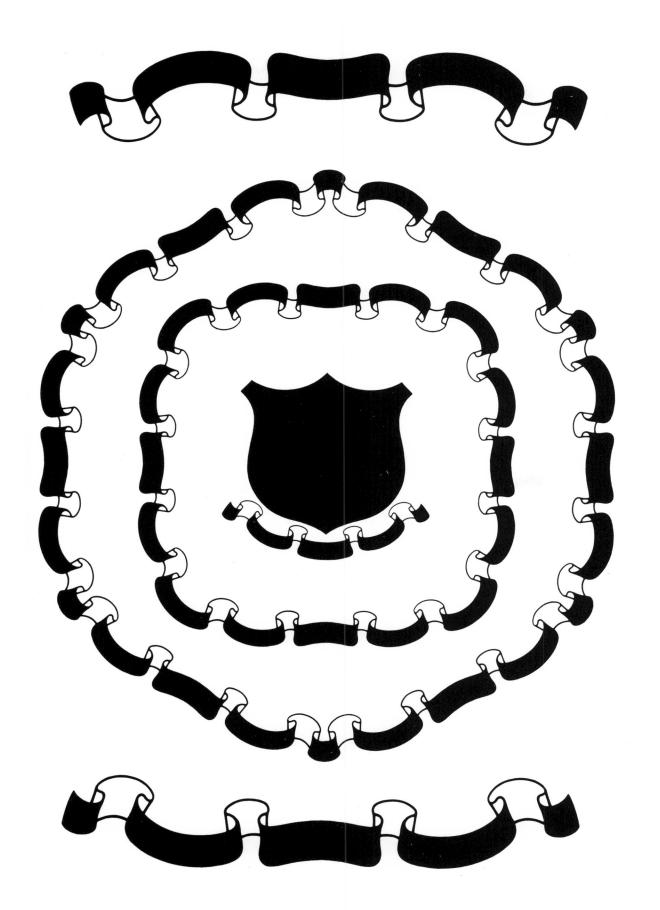

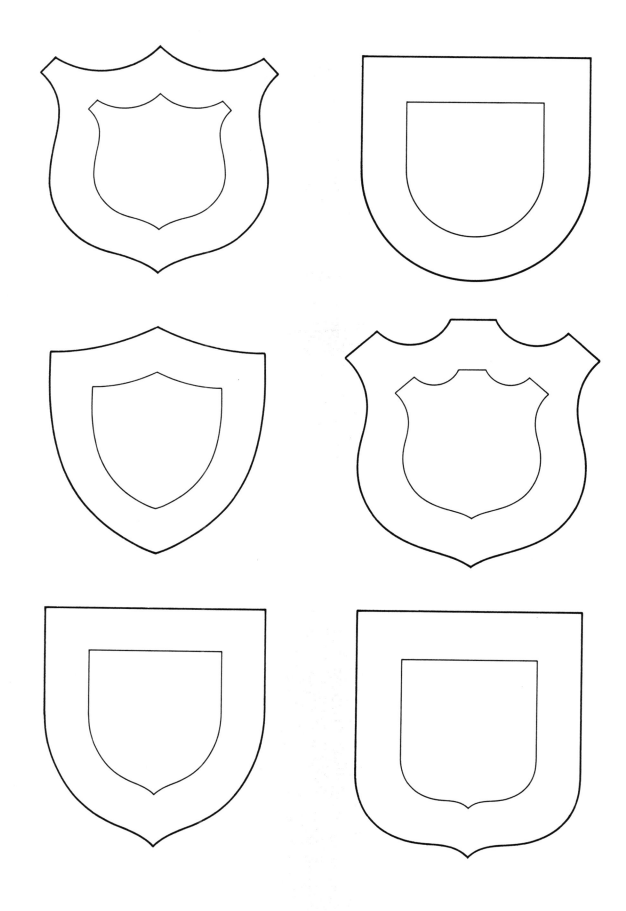

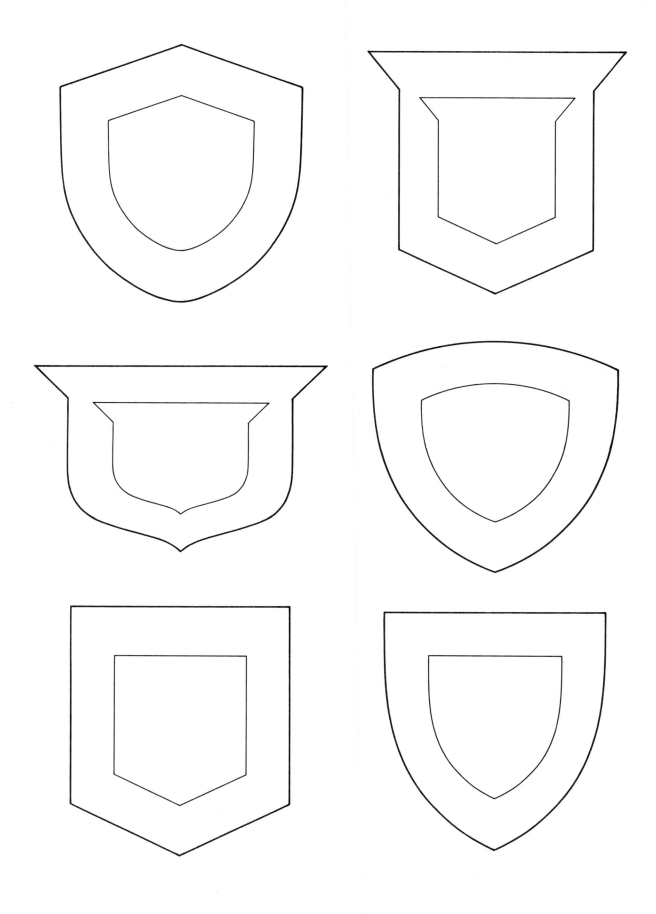

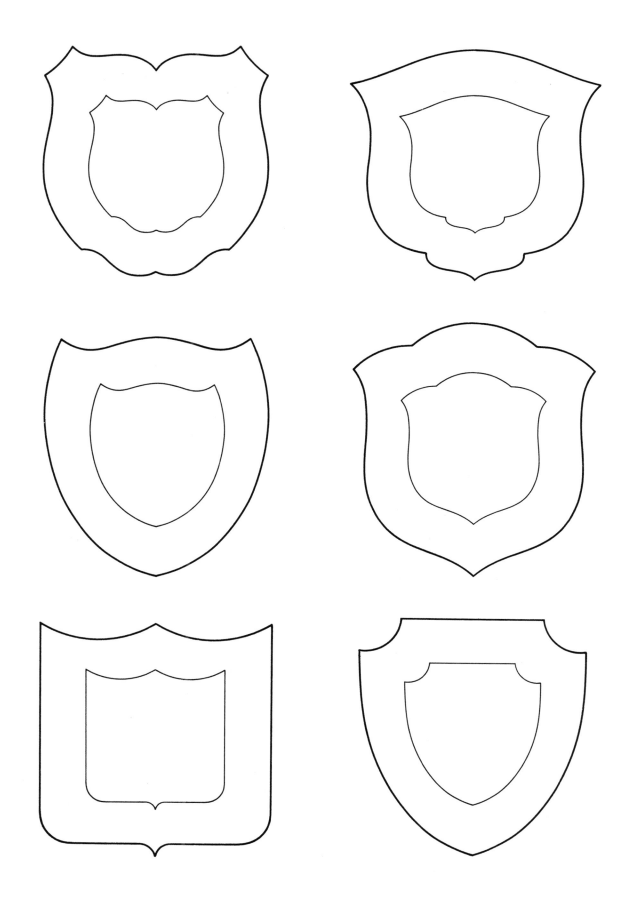

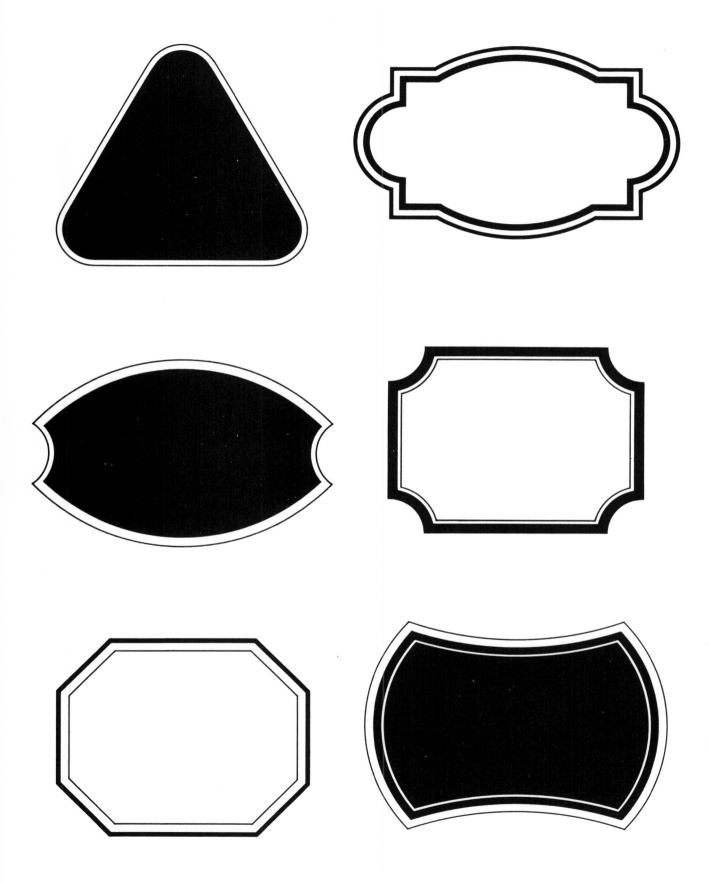

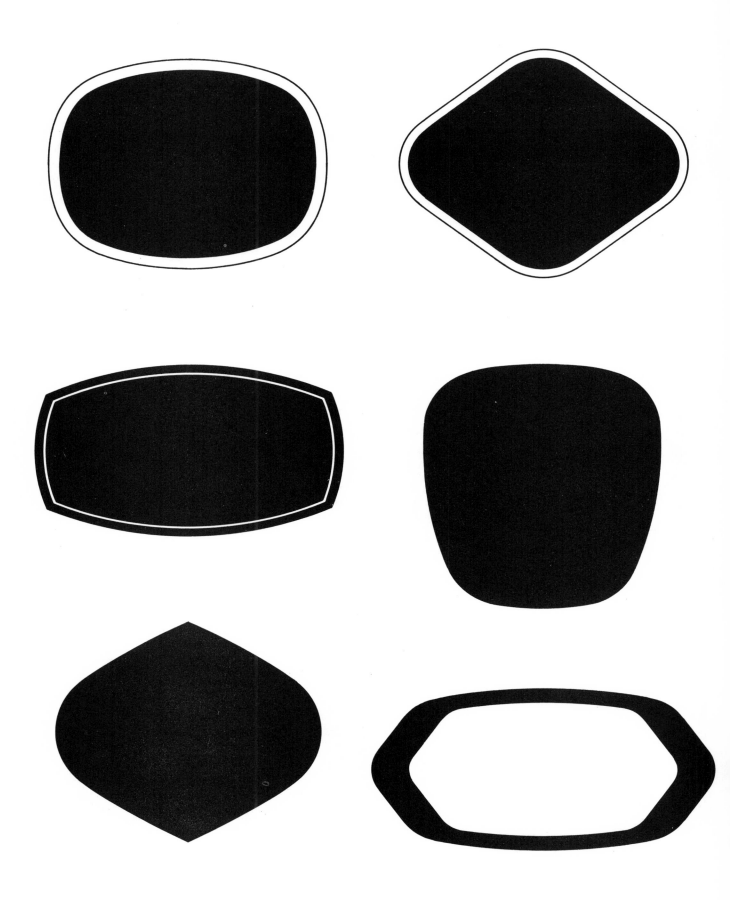

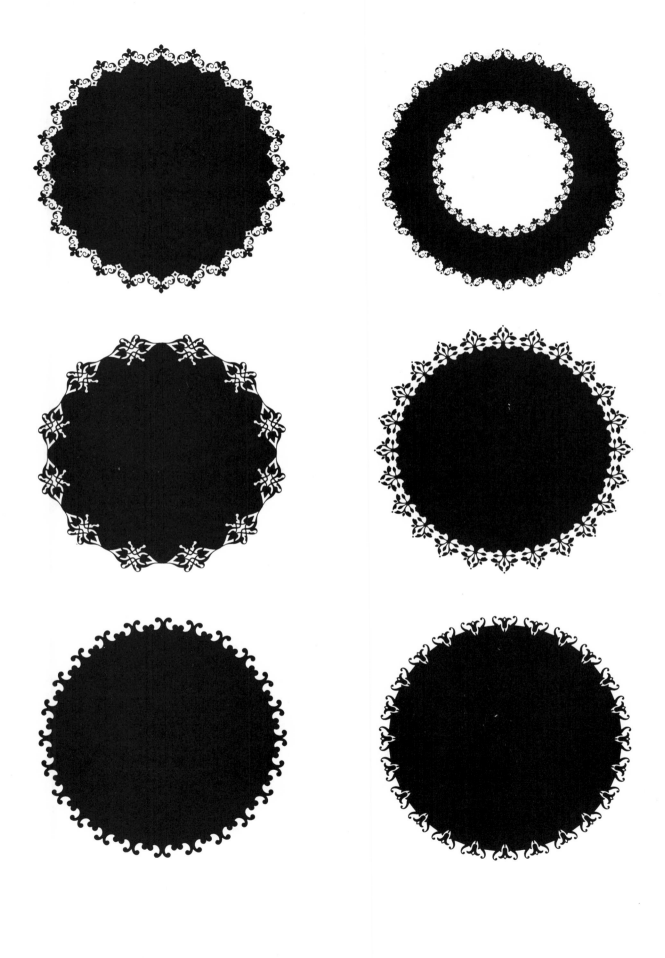

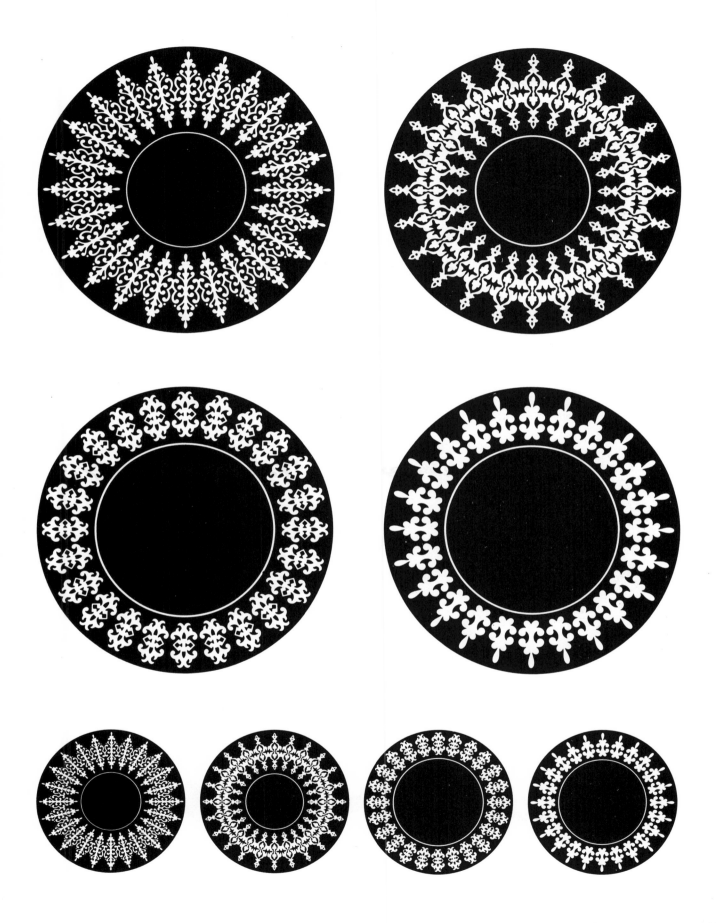

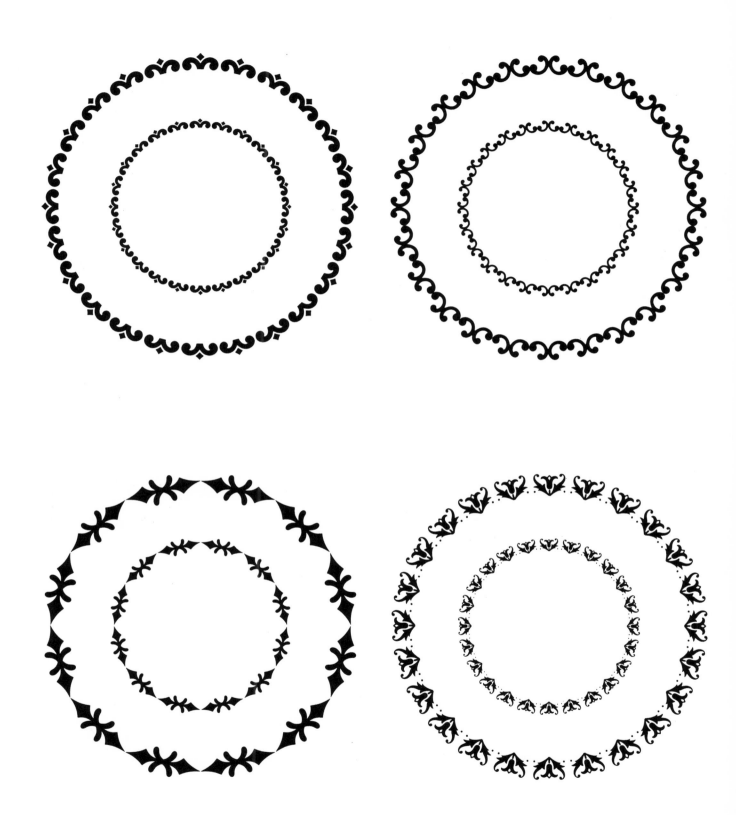

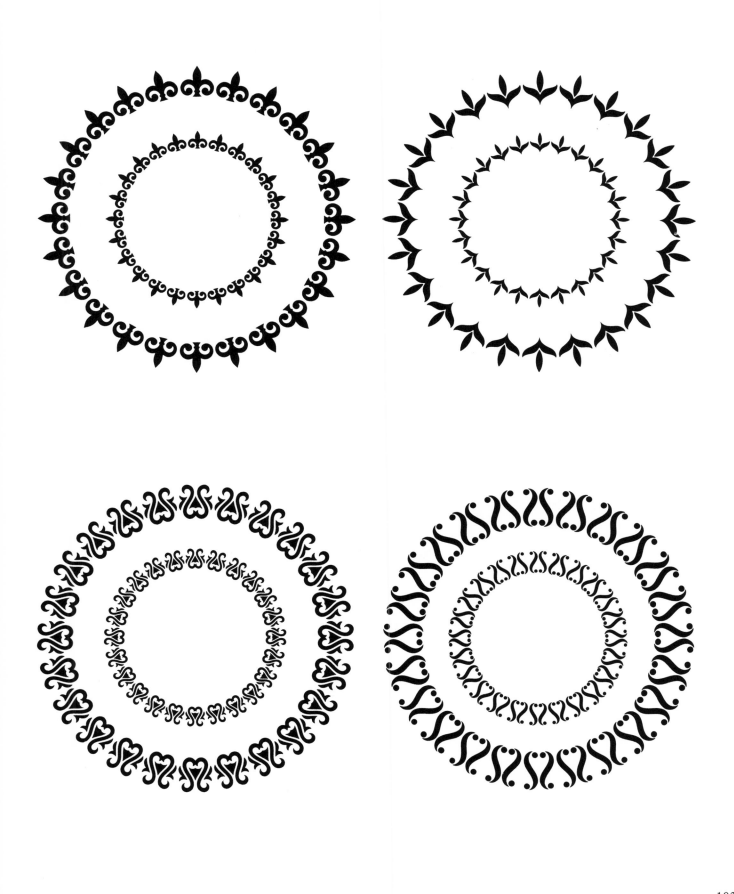

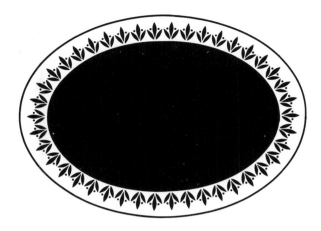
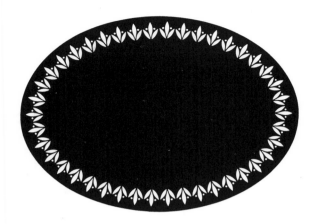

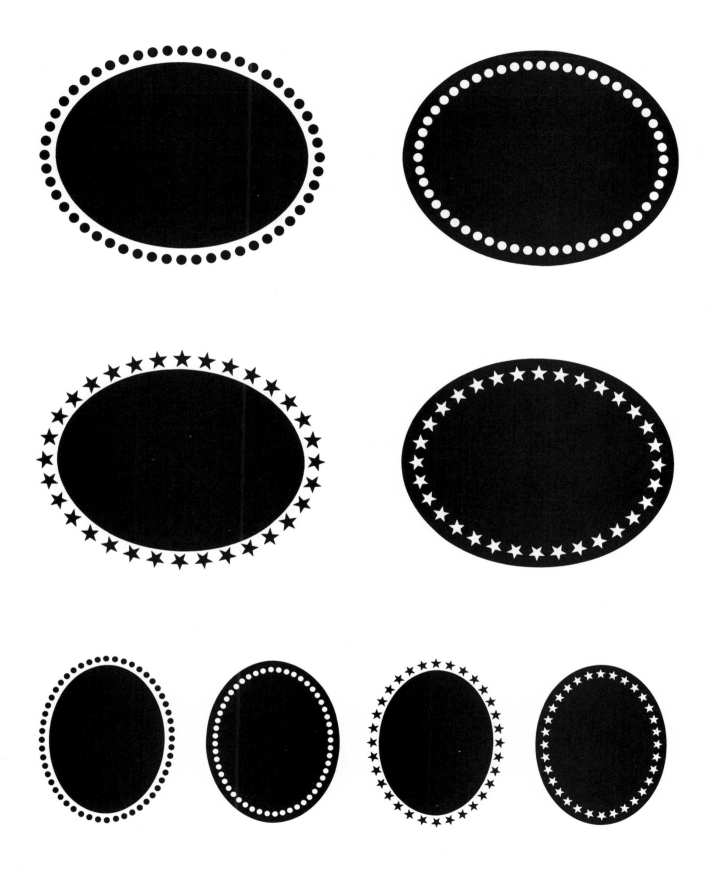

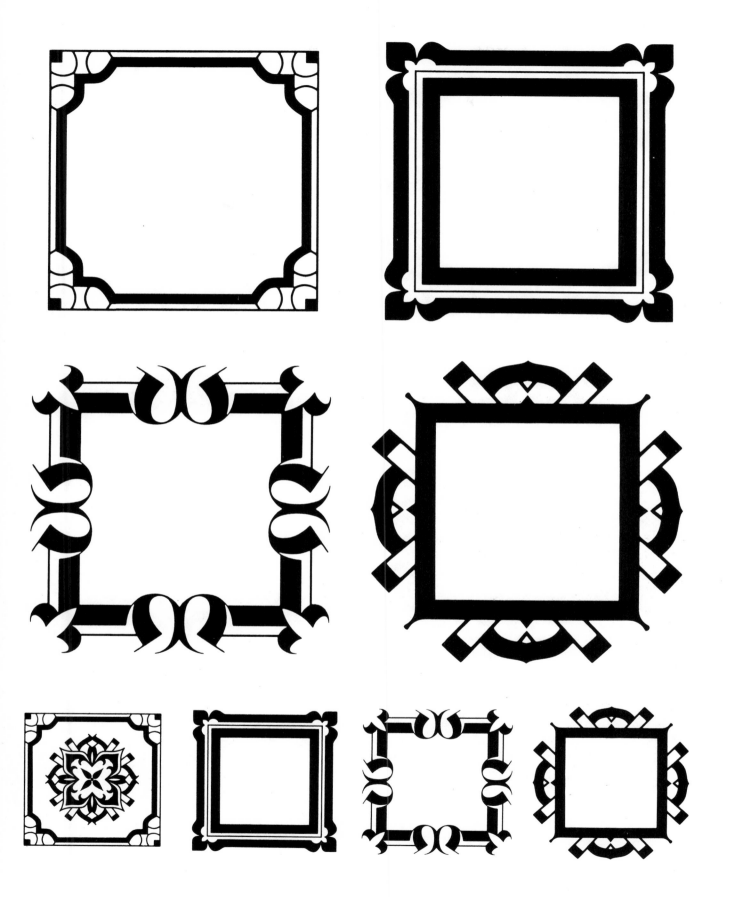

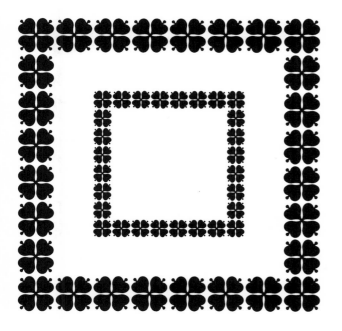

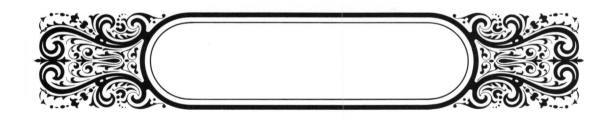

131

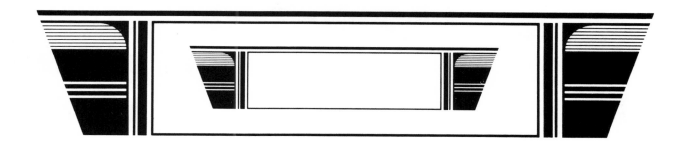

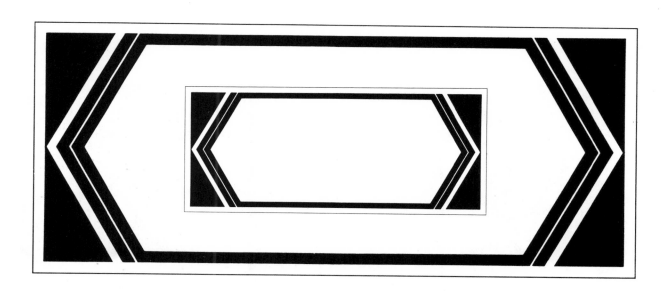

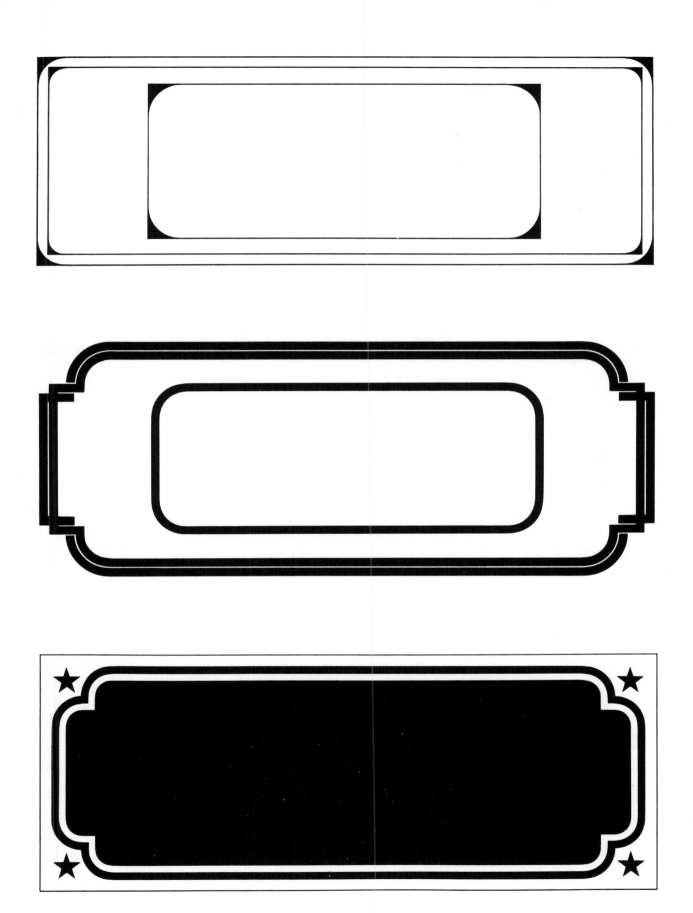

141

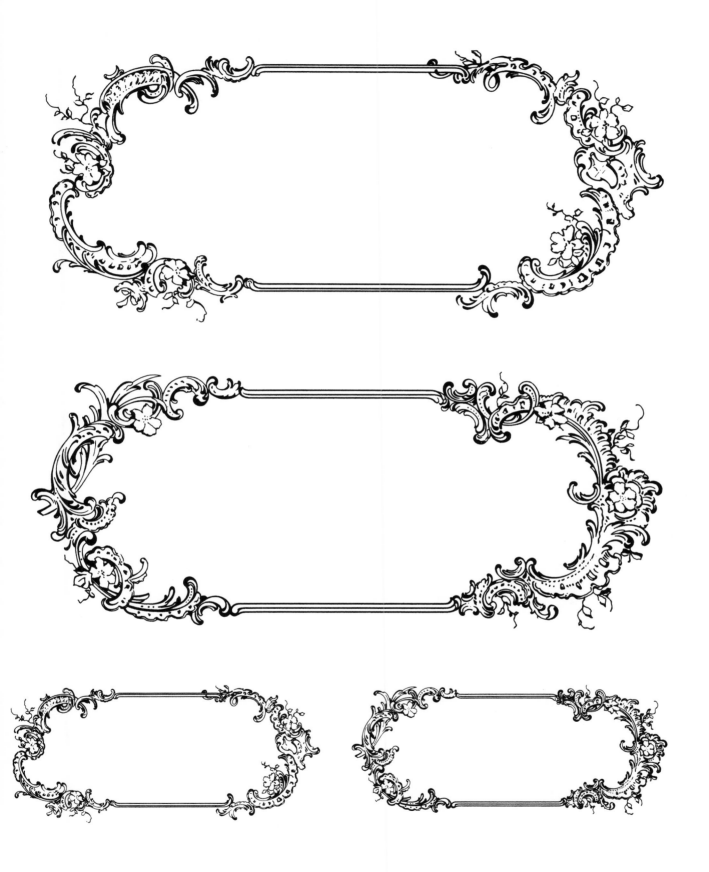

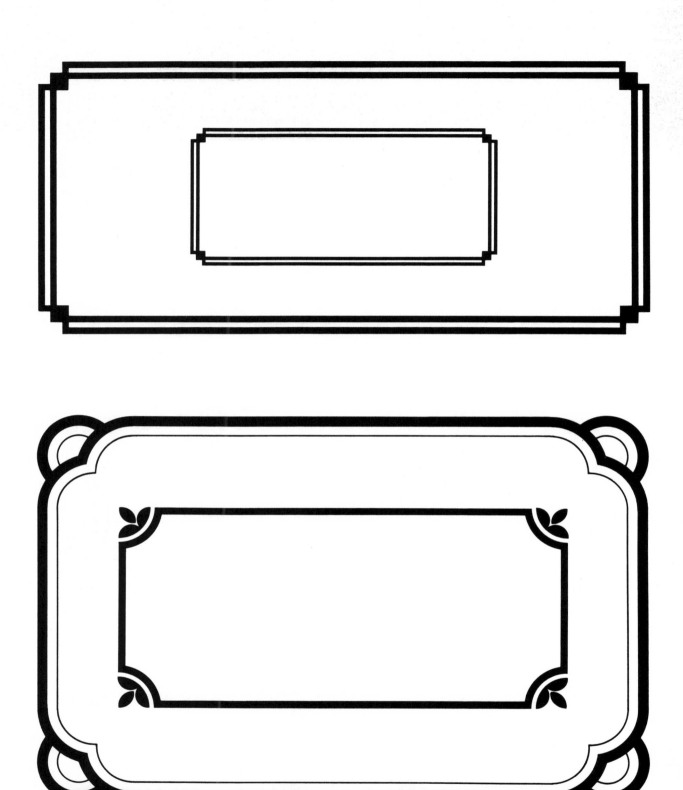

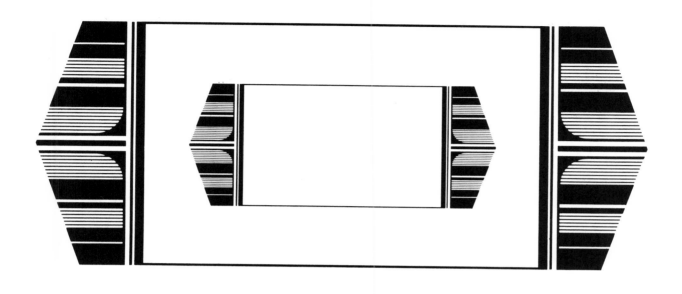

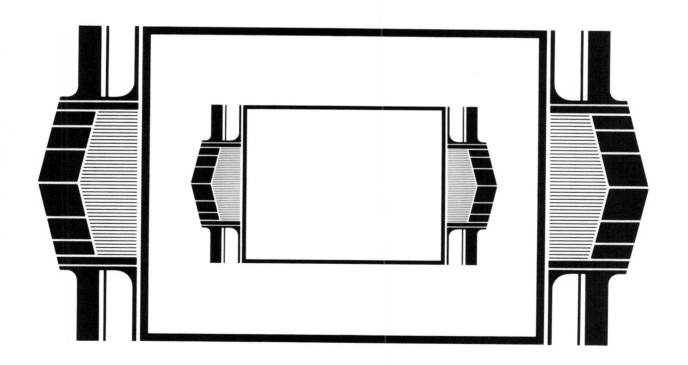

145

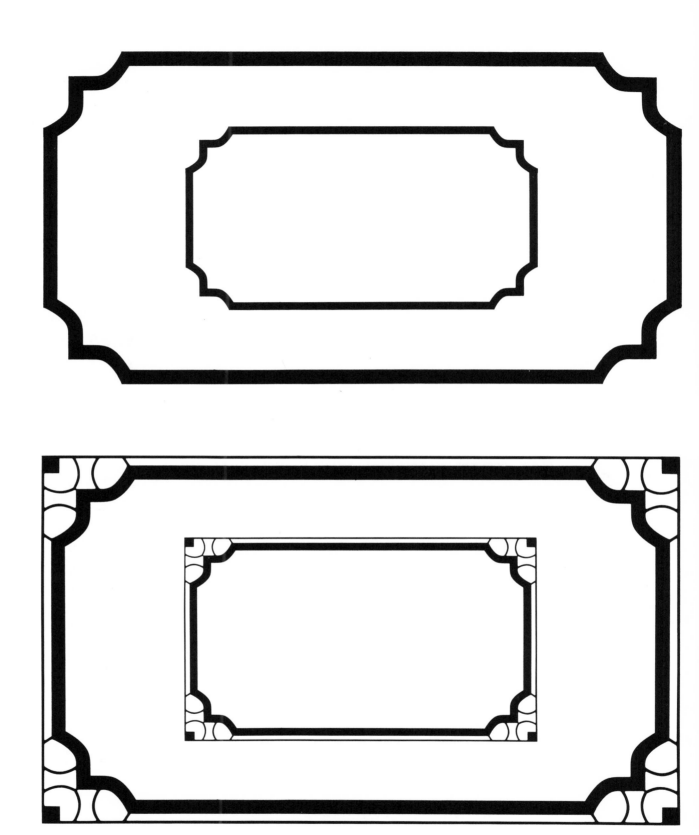

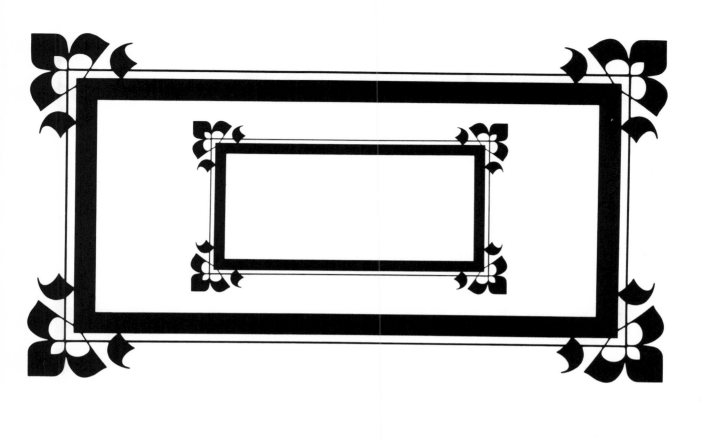

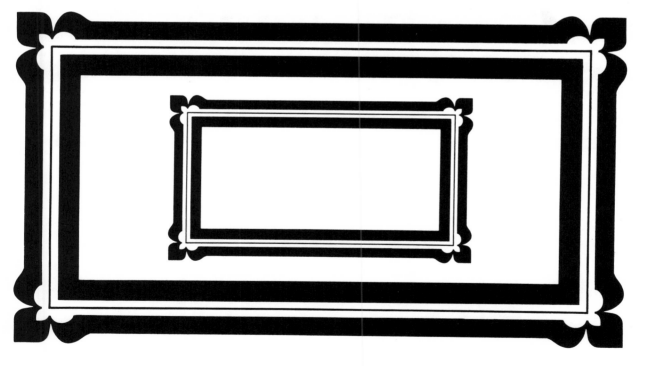

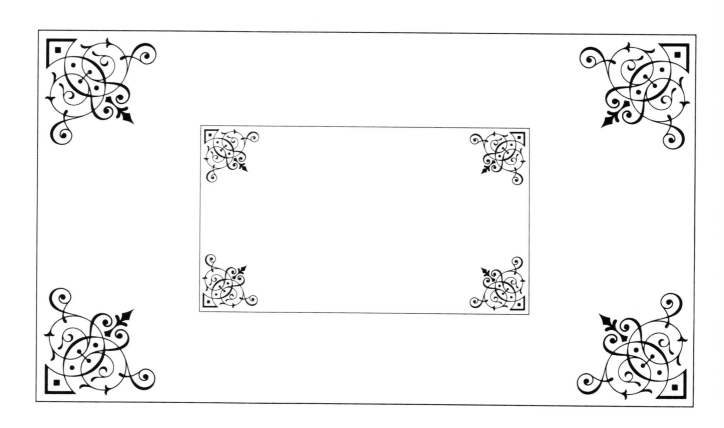

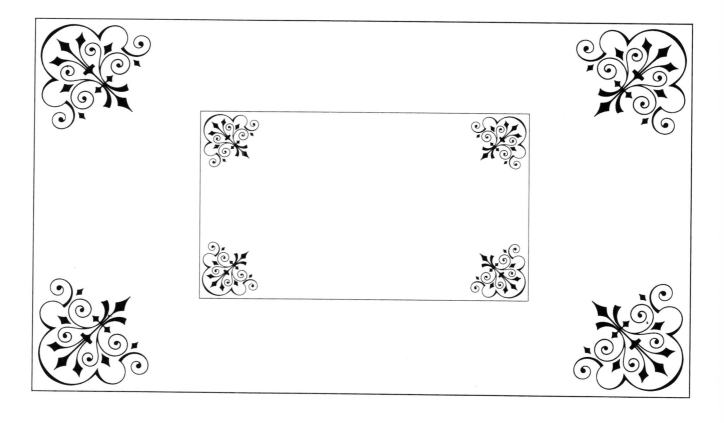

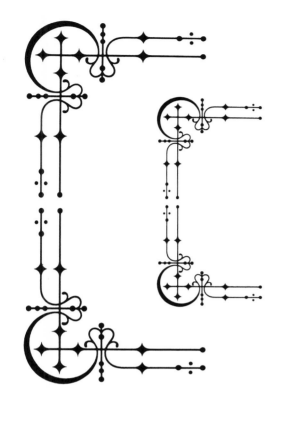

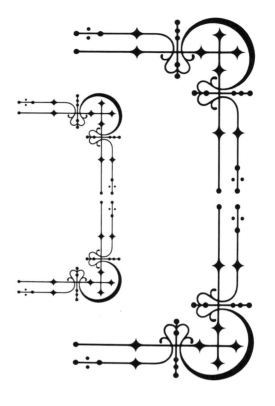

154

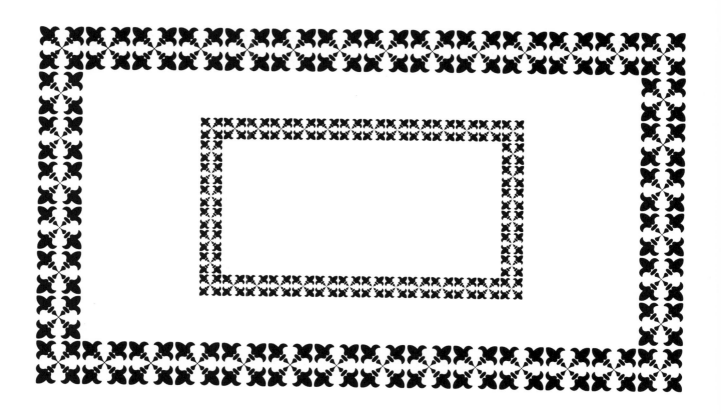

158

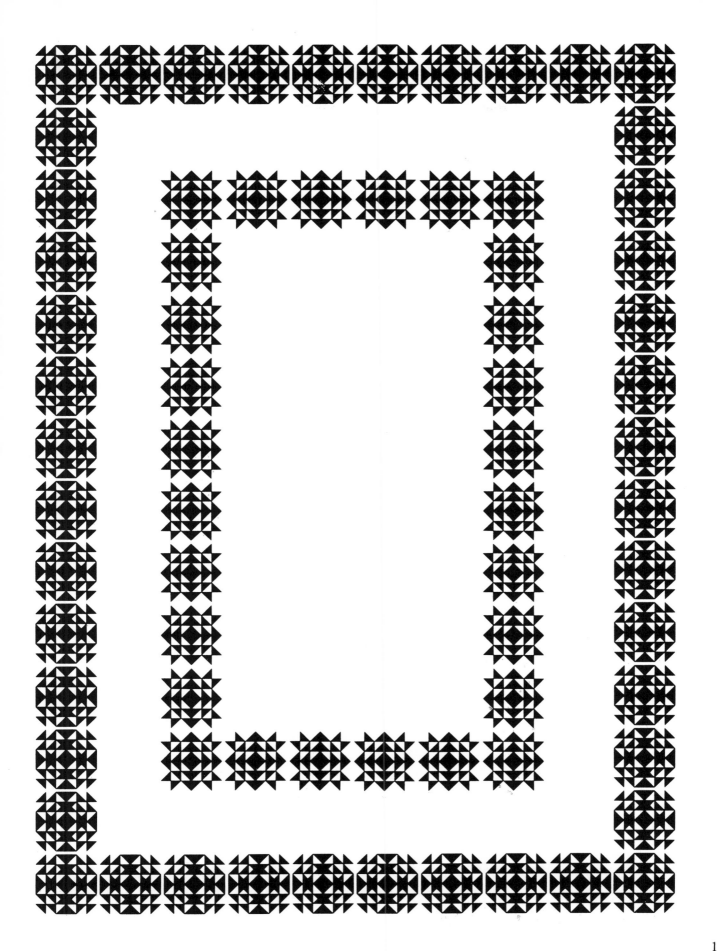

163

164

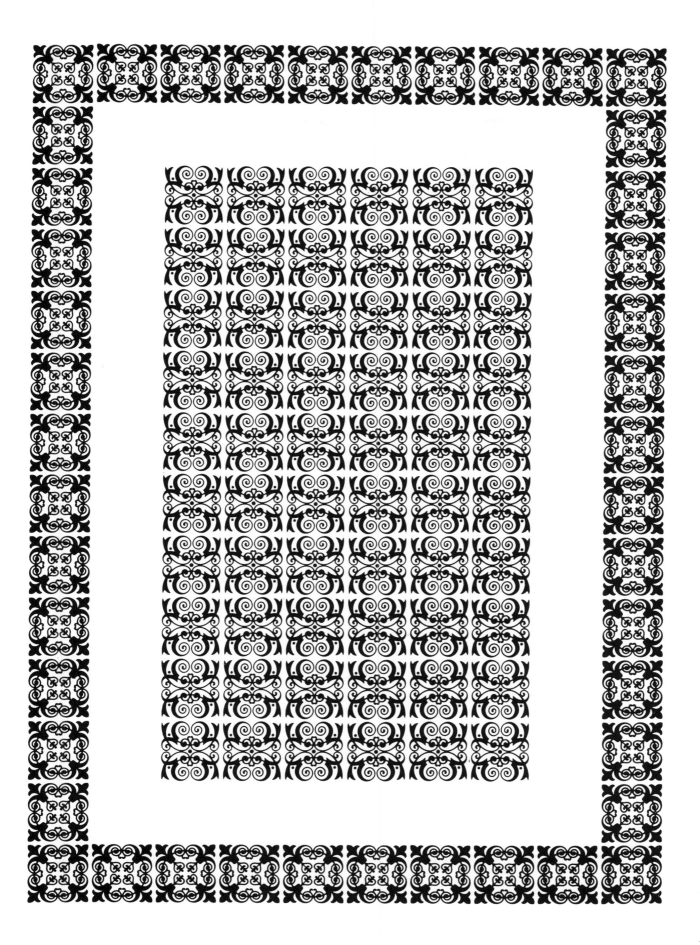

166

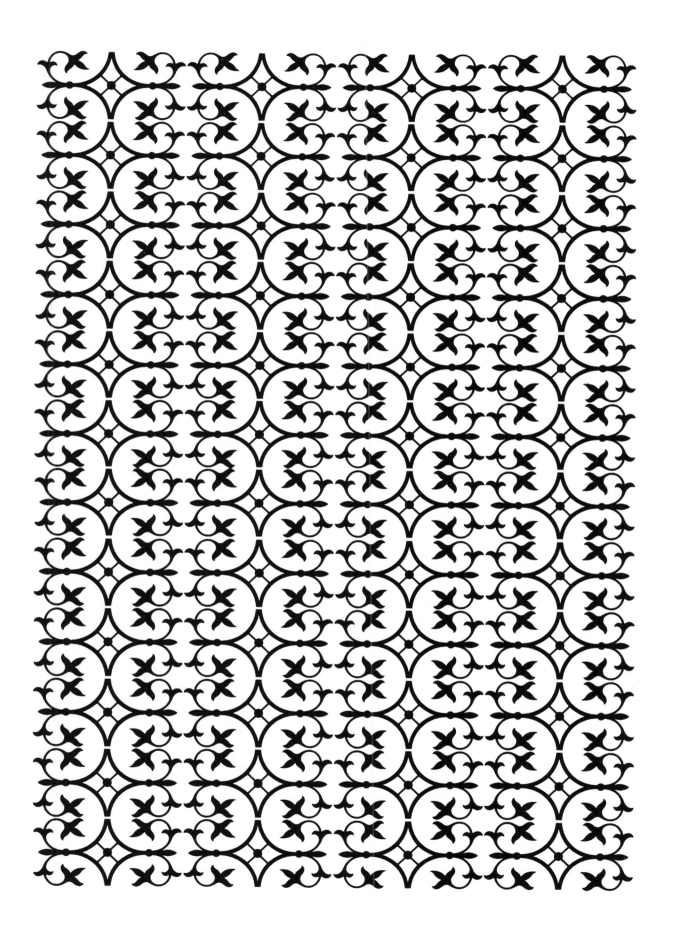

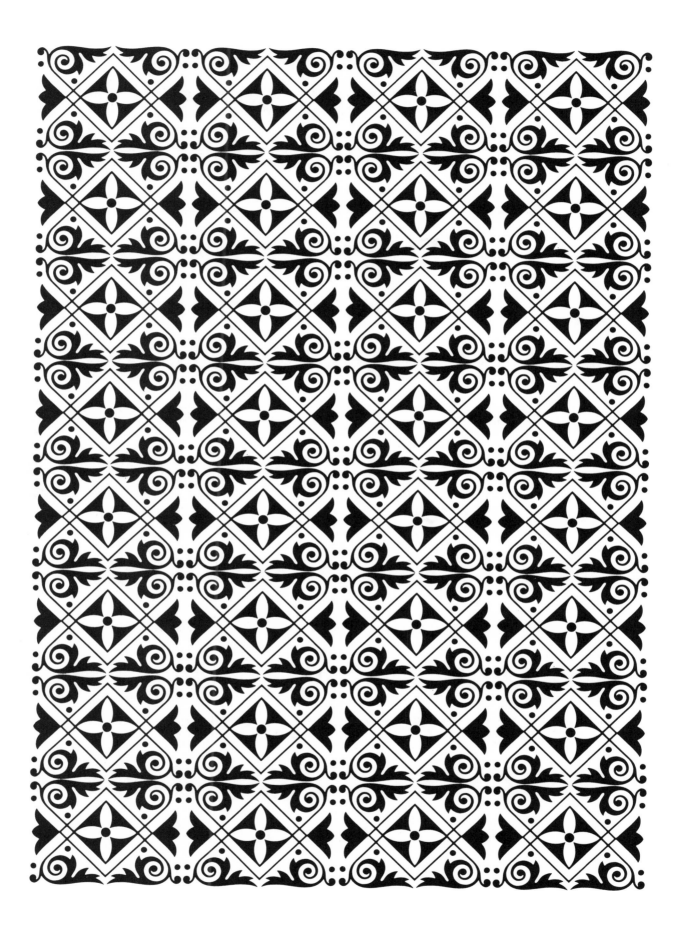

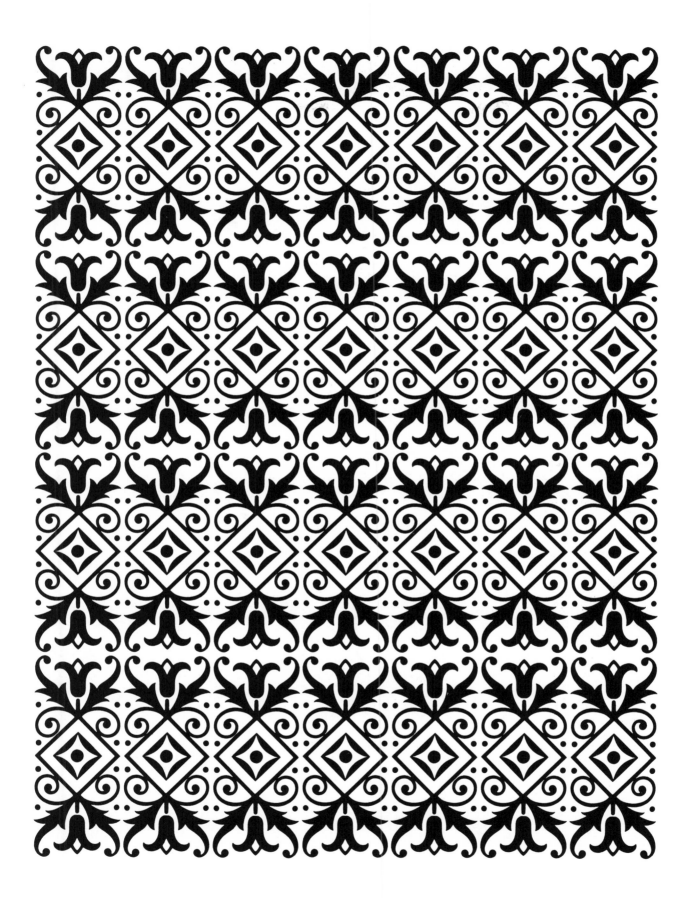